Srinishnu

ELLIS ISLAND

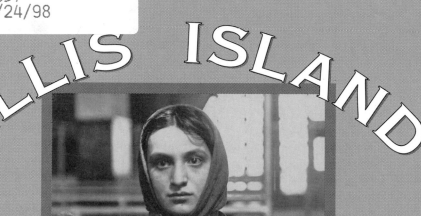

A TRUE BOOK

by
Patricia Ryon Quiri

Children's Press®
A Division of Grolier Publishing

New York London Hong Kong Sydney
Danbury, Connecticut

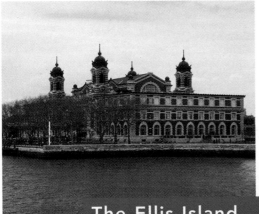

The Ellis Island
Immigration Center

Reading Consultant
Linda Cornwell
Learning Resource Consultant
Indiana Department
of Education

*Author's Dedication:
For Marian Lomurro Sheridan,
my wonderful friend of thirty-
two years. Much love, Pitter*

Visit Children's Press on the Internet at:
http://publishing.grolier.com

Library of Congress Cataloging-in-Publication Data

Quiri, Patricia Ryon.
    Ellis Island: a true book / Patricia Ryon Quiri.
        p.   cm. — (True book)
    Includes bibliographical references (p.) and index.
    Summary: Describes how the immigration station at Ellis Island served
as a gateway into the United states for millions of immigrants.
    ISBN 0-516-20622-2 (lib.bdg.)   0-516-26374-9 (pbk.)
    1. Ellis Island Immigration Station (New York, N.Y.)—Juvenile litera-
ture. 2. Ellis Island (N.Y)—History—Juvenile literature. 3. United
States—Emigration and immigration—History—Juvenile literature.
[1. Ellis Island Immigration Station (New York, N.Y.)—History. 2. United
States—Emigration and immigration.] I. Title. II. Series.
JV6484.Q57   1998
325.73—dc21   97-9356
                                                                 CIP
                                                                  AC

Contents

Italian immigrants at Ellis Island in 1905

Moving Families

Moving to a new place can be exciting. The thought of making new friends and going to a new school is exciting. But it can also be frightening. Many questions go through the minds of people who move. What will the new place be like? Will I make new friends easily?

Today, families often move to different cities and different states. Sometimes families even move to different countries.

In the late 1890s and into the 1900s, many families from Europe decided to move to the United States. Europe was crowded. Many of the people were very poor. Some people wanted religious freedom. Others wanted political freedom.

Immigrants on a ship bound for New York

They left relatives, friends, and jobs to come to the United States. Such a big change was frightening for them, but they felt life would be much better if they moved. They had heard wonderful stories about life in the United States.

The people who decided to leave their countries to settle in the United States were called immigrants. Many immigrants thought that the United States was the land of riches and opportunity.

A Rough Journey

The immigrants crossed the Atlantic Ocean in steamships. It was a difficult journey. Most immigrants had little money. Saving ten dollars for one steerage ticket took months, sometimes years. Steerage is the basement of a steamship. Imagine spending three weeks

Steerage quarters were dirty and over-crowded (above). Sometimes, steerage passengers were allowed to get some fresh air on the deck of the ship (right).

in a cold, crowded, dark base-ment! That's how long it took to cross the Atlantic Ocean.

Other immigrants were luckier. They had enough money to buy first- or second-class tickets for the upper decks of the ship. These people were able to see the Statue of Liberty as they came into New York Harbor.

The Statue of Liberty was a symbol of hope and freedom to the immigrants. This statue,

The Statue of Liberty greets visitors to New York Harbor.

located on what was then called Bedloe's Island, greeted the millions of immigrants who entered the United States over the years.

First- and second-class passengers were asked lots of questions on the ship just before entering the United States. Steerage or third-class passengers had to go through a more complicated process before being allowed to enter the country. They were taken by barge to a small island

called Ellis Island. On Ellis Island, these immigrants had to face questions and medical exams.

Sometimes immigrants had to wait several days on the steamships before getting on the barge. That was because there were so many immigrants coming into the country.

Ellis Island

Hundreds of years ago, American Indians went to Ellis Island for oysters and clams. They called it Kioshk, or Gull Island, because so many birds hunted the oysters.

Over the years, the island had many different names. In the 1770s, a merchant and fisherman named Samuel Ellis became the owner of the island. It was after Mr. Ellis that the island was named. The name stuck through the years.

Many years after Sam Ellis's death, the island was taken over by the United States government. The government used the island as a place to store ammunition. The island was also used as a place to execute pirates.

On April 11, 1890, President Benjamin Harrison signed an important paper stating that all ammunition should be removed from Ellis Island. The island was going to be the new immigration center for the United States.

Its location in New York Harbor was perfect. The federal government built a beautiful large wooden building on the island. This building would process the thousands

The original immigration center built on Ellis Island

of immigrants who came to the United States every week.

Ellis Island Opens

The immigration center on Ellis Island opened on January 1, 1892. More than two thousand people came through on that first day. It was there that the immigrants would find out if they would be allowed to stay in the United States.

Immigrants arriving
at Ellis Island

A statue of Annie Moore, the first immigrant to register at Ellis Island

The very first immigrant to be registered at the new immigration center was an Irish girl named Annie Moore. She was fifteen years old. Immigration officials gave her a ten-dollar gold piece as a prize for being the first to pass through Ellis Island's doors.

For the next five years, thousands of immigrants passed through the immigration center. Annie Moore and every other immigrant had to go through medical examinations and questions. The immigrants had to wait in long lines.

The Immigration Center Burns

Five years after the immigration center opened, a huge fire raced through the wooden buildings at Ellis Island. The water around the island was too shallow for tugboats to put out the fire. The buildings burned to the ground. Luckily, no one died. the immigrants

A new, bigger immigration center was built after the fire of 1897.

Immigrants who spent more than a few hours at Ellis Island were given a meal.

had been taken safely off the burning island.

Ellis Island's immigration center was rebuilt. This time, iron and brick were used to construct the buildings. Landfill was used to make the island larger. By this time, Ellis Island was 17 acres (7 hectares). The new main building looked like a beautiful palace. Other buildings included a kitchen and dining room, a hospital, a bathhouse, and a laundry building.

The Isle of Tears

Going through Ellis Island was an experience that no immigrant forgot. The process usually took three to five hours. When the immigrants went into the main building, they dropped off their bags in the baggage area. Sometimes the baggage area was so full that people lost their belongings.

Immigrants in front of the main building at Ellis Island (above) and an exhibit showing baggage carried by people who passed through Ellis Island (right)

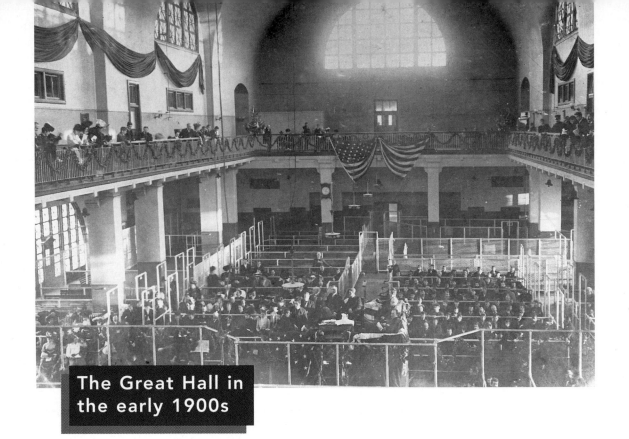

The Great Hall in
the early 1900s

Next they went up a large
staircase to get to the Great
Hall, or registry room. When
they finally got upstairs, doctors checked them for diseases.
The medical examiners wanted

to make sure the immigrants wouldn't bring any contagious diseases into the United States. The doctors also wanted to make sure that the immigrants were strong and healthy enough to make a living in America.

A doctor examining an immigrant at Ellis Island

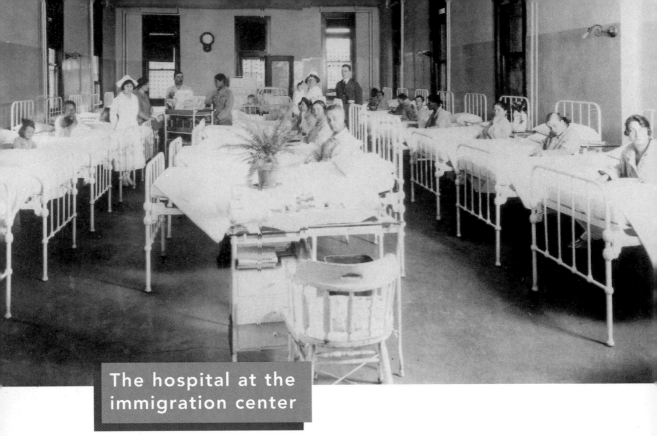

The hospital at the immigration center

If a problem was found, the immigrant's clothing was marked with a letter. "H" meant heart disease. "X" meant mental problems. "E" meant eye problems. If a disease could be cured, the immigrant was sent to the hospital on the island.

If immigrants passed the medical exam, they were given a legal exam. This was a bunch of questions. They were asked if they had money for a train ticket. They were asked where they came from and where they planned to go in the United States. In later years at Ellis Island, immigrants were asked if they could read and write.

Immigrants being questioned in the Great Hall

If they passed the legal exam, immigrants were given a landing card. This meant they could enter the United States. They went back downstairs. They could exchange their foreign money and they could buy a train ticket if they needed one.

There was a post office on the first floor. There was also a telegraph office. Finally, the

Immigrants waiting to exchange their money for American dollars

immigrants picked up their baggage. They were ready to begin their new lives in the United States of America!

Some immigrants were not allowed to stay in the country. These were people who had contagious diseases or who could not prove that they'd be able to support themselves in the United States. Sometimes, some members of a family were allowed to stay while others were sent back home. About

Immigrants leaving Ellis Island

two percent of the total number of immigrants through the years were sent back to their original countries. That was about 250,000 people. That was why Ellis Island was sometimes called the "Isle of Tears."

A Gateway for Millions

Twelve million people were processed at Ellis Island. Nearly forty percent of the people living in the United States today had immigrant relatives who went through Ellis Island.

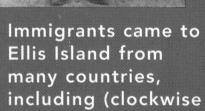

Immigrants came to Ellis Island from many countries, including (clockwise from top right) the Ukraine, Romania, Finland, and Guadeloupe.

Ellis Island Closes

In 1921, Congress passed a new immigration law. It limited the number of immigrants allowed into the United States. It also limited the number of immigrants allowed in from each country. This was called a quota system. The number of immigrants coming into the United States dropped greatly.

After it closed, the immigration center fell into disrepair.

Because of this, Ellis Island was no longer needed. On November 29, 1954, the federal government closed the island.

Over the years, the buildings became ruined. Ellis Island stayed empty until 1965, when President Lyndon B. Johnson put the National Park Service in charge of the island.

New Museum

Ellis Island had been a symbol of the American dream. It represented hope and freedom. Millions of courageous people came to the United States in search of a better life. These immigrants built the United States into a powerful country.

The Great Hall during (above) and after (right) its restoration

Because of this, the government decided to make Ellis Island a national monument. Millions of dollars were spent fixing up the island and its buildings and turning them into a museum.

On September 10, 1990, the Ellis Island Immigration Museum opened. The museum educates visitors about the immigrant experience. It is a

The Ellis Island Immigration Museum opened in 1990.

self-guided tour that includes movies, many exhibits, artifacts, music, and photographs.

The restored Great Hall

The United States has been a nation of immigrants seeking the American dream. For some, Ellis Island was the Isle of Tears, but for the great majority, it was the Isle of Hope.

To Find Out More

Here are some additional resources to help you learn more about Ellis Island:

 **Books**

Jacobs, William Jay. **Ellis Island: New Hope in a New Land.** Charles Scribner's Sons, 1990.

Levine, Ellen. **If Your Name Was Changed at Ellis Island. . .** Scholastic Inc., 1993.

Maestro, Betsy. **Coming to America.** Scholastic Inc., 1996.

Stein, R. Conrad. **The Story of Ellis Island.** Children's Press, 1992.

Tifft, Wilton S. **Ellis Island.** Contemporary Books, 1990.

💡 Organizations and Online Sites

Great Outdoor Recreation Pages (GORP): Statue of Liberty National Monument
http://www.gorp.com/gorp/resource/US_nm/ny_liber.htm

History of Ellis Island and the Statue of Liberty, visitor information, and lots of links.

Hot Links: Statue of Liberty and Ellis Island
http://www.ellisisland.org/hotlinks.html

Great links to sites related to the Statue of Liberty and Ellis Island.

Statue of Liberty National Monument and Ellis Island
Liberty Island
New York, NY 10004
http://www.nps.gov/stli

This organization runs two exciting places to visit: the Ellis Island Immigration Museum and the Statue of Liberty. Its website offers information about the Ellis Island Immigration Museum, as well as history, stories, statistics, and photographs about Ellis Island and the Statue of Liberty.

Important Words

ammunition explosive material used in weapons

artifacts objects having historical value

contagious diseases diseases that can be passed from one person to another

examination inspection

execute to put to death

exhibit display

foreign from a country different from one's own

landfill soil, trash, or garbage used to build up low land

majority the greater number of something

quota a set number or amount

Index

Meet the Author

Patricia Ryon Quiri lives in Palm Harbor, Florida, with her husband Bob and three sons. She is a graduate of Alfred University in upstate New York and has a B.A. in elementary education. Ms. Quiri currently teaches second grade in the Pinellas County school system. Other True Books by Ms. Quiri include *The Bald Eagle*, *The American Flag*, *The National Anthem*, and *The Statue of Liberty*.